FAMILY ROOTS RUN DEEP, LIKE A TREE PLANTED IN...

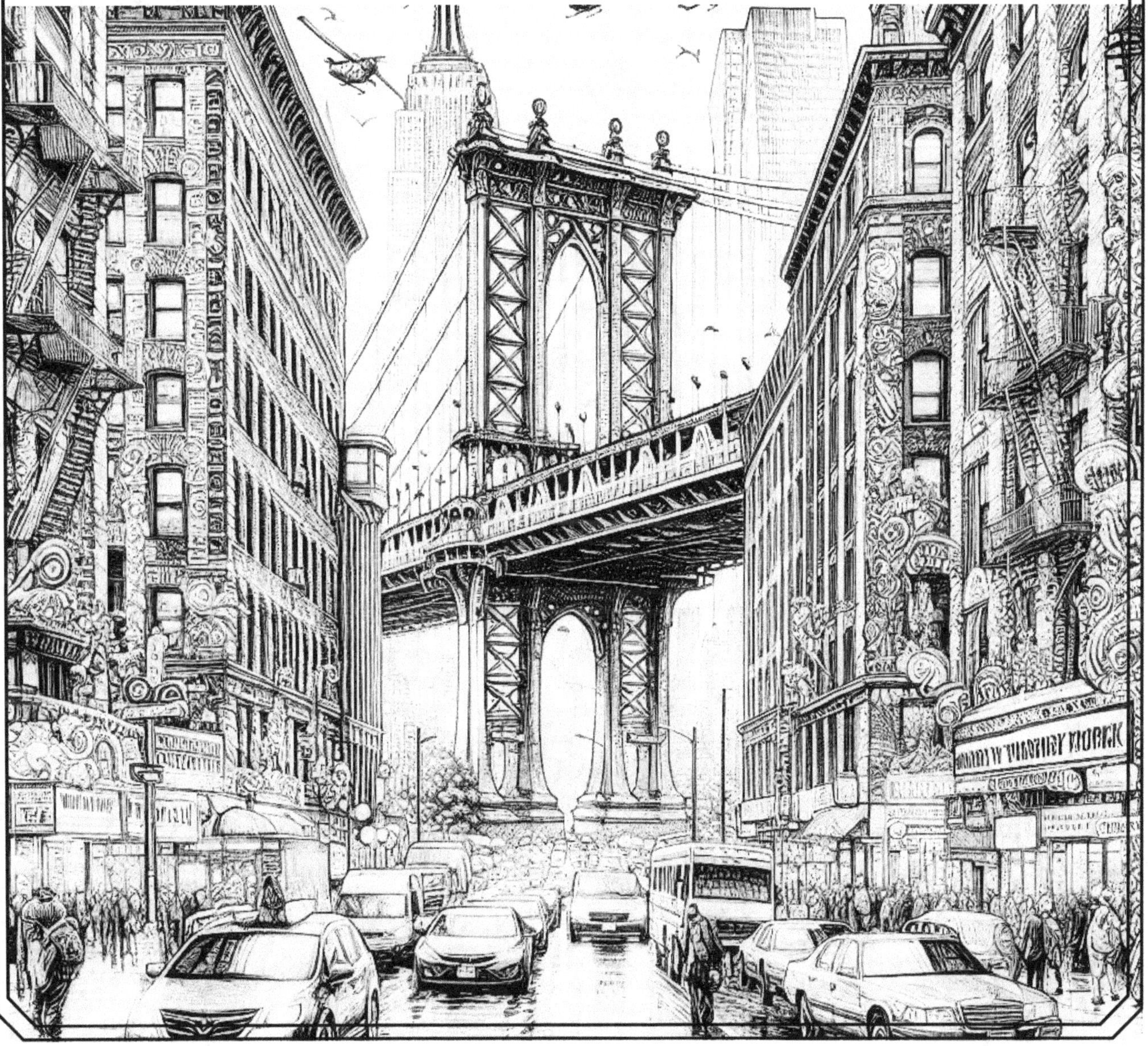

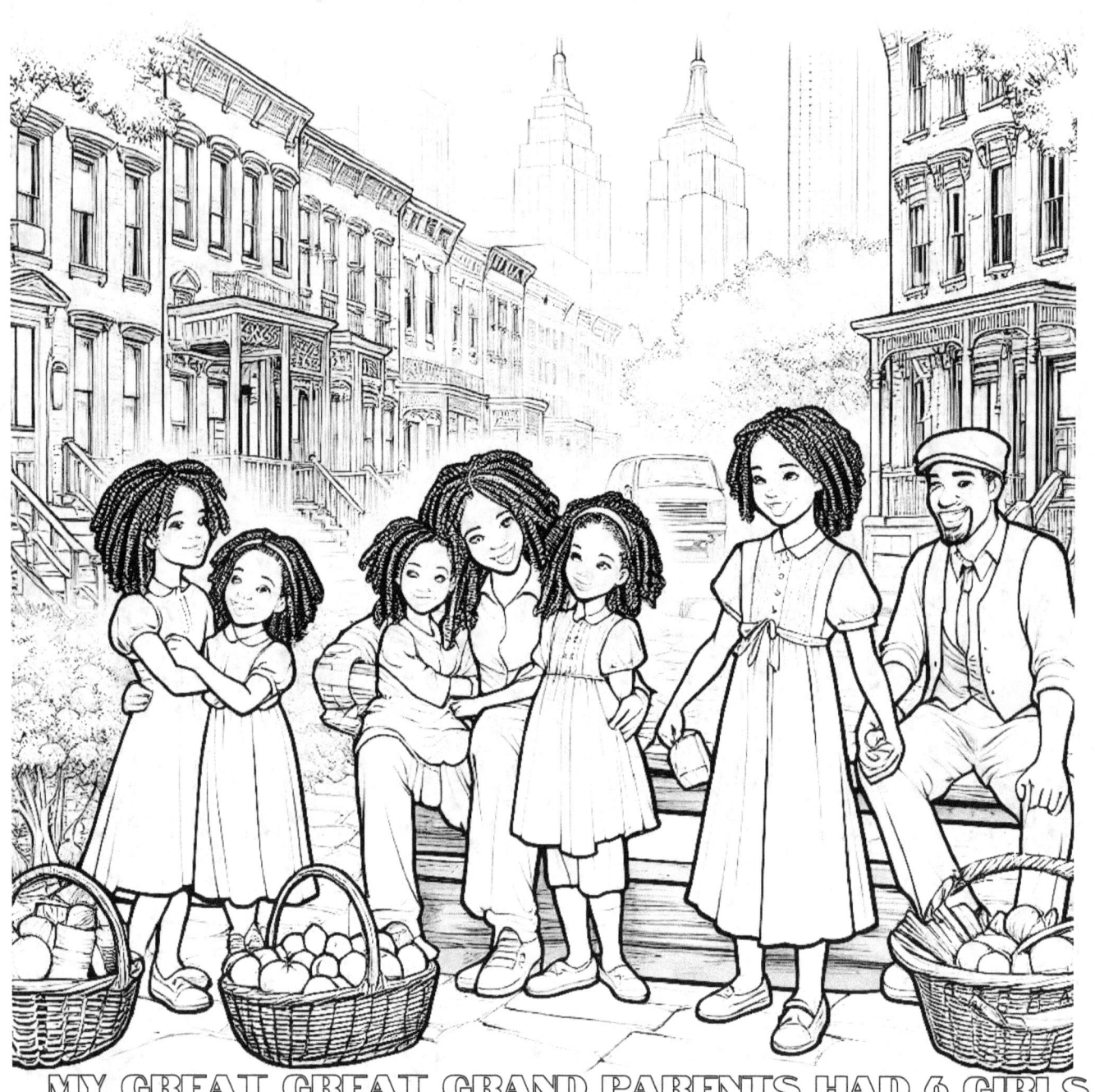

MY GREAT GREAT GRAND PARENTS HAD 6 GIRLS

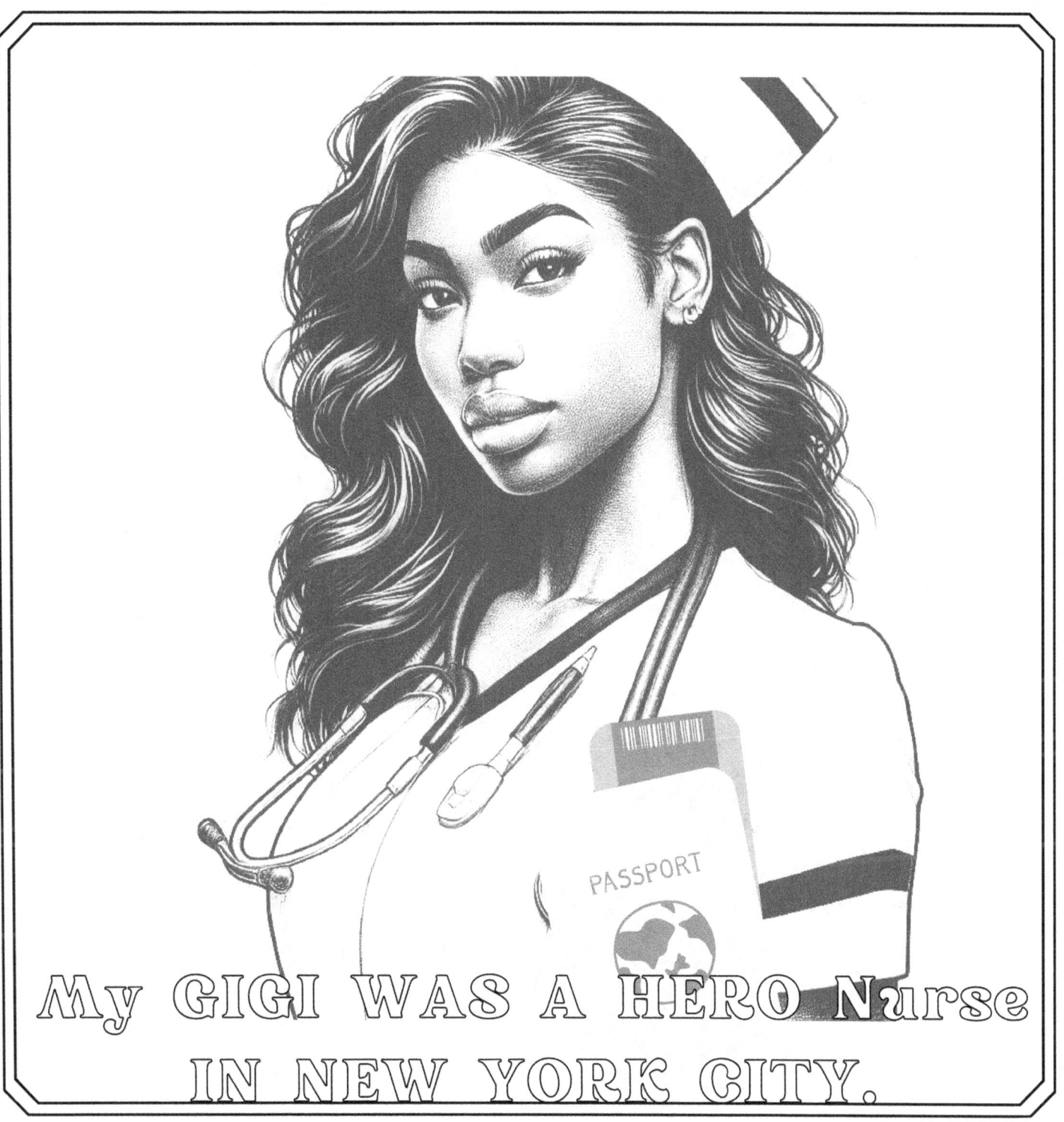

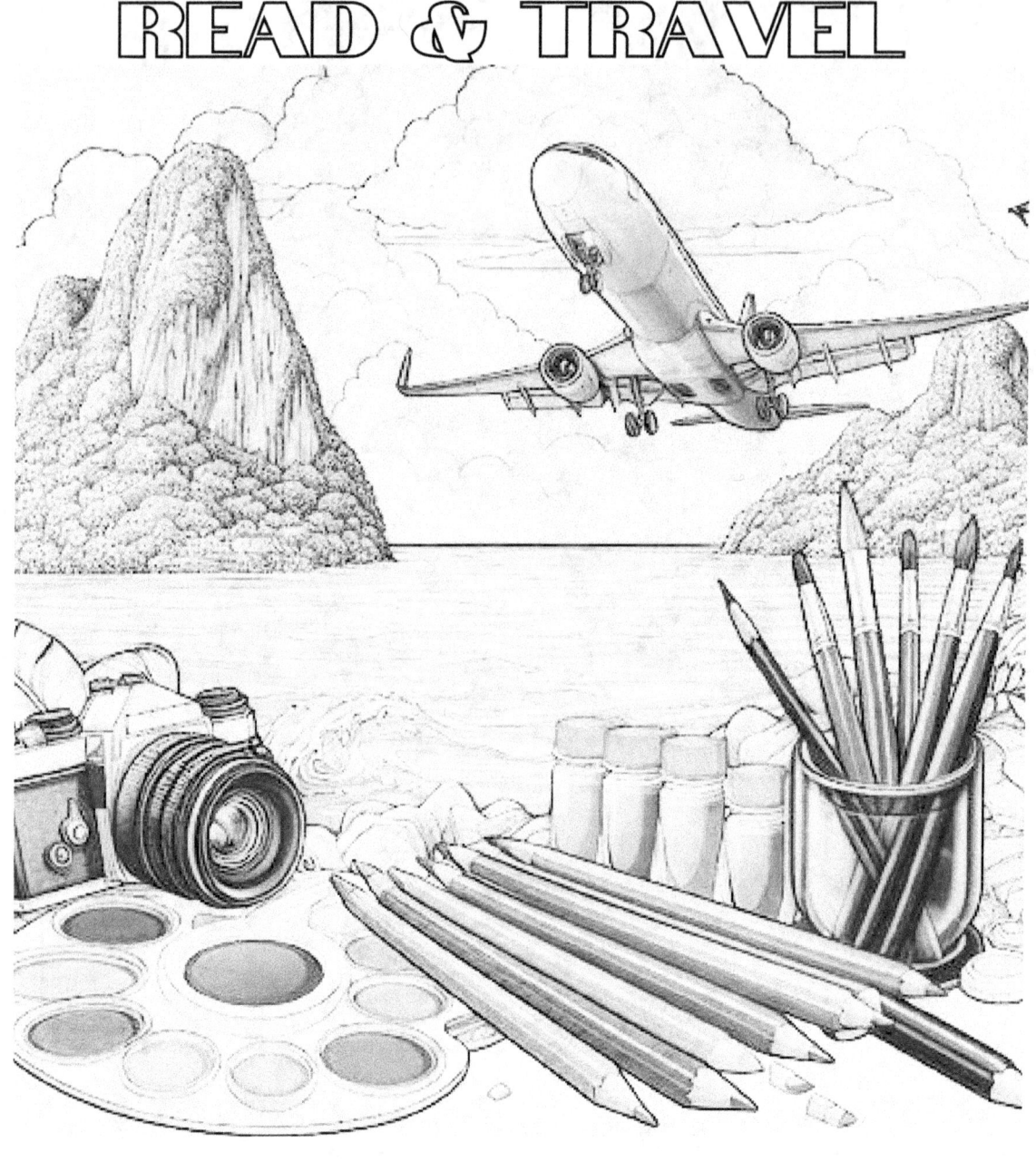

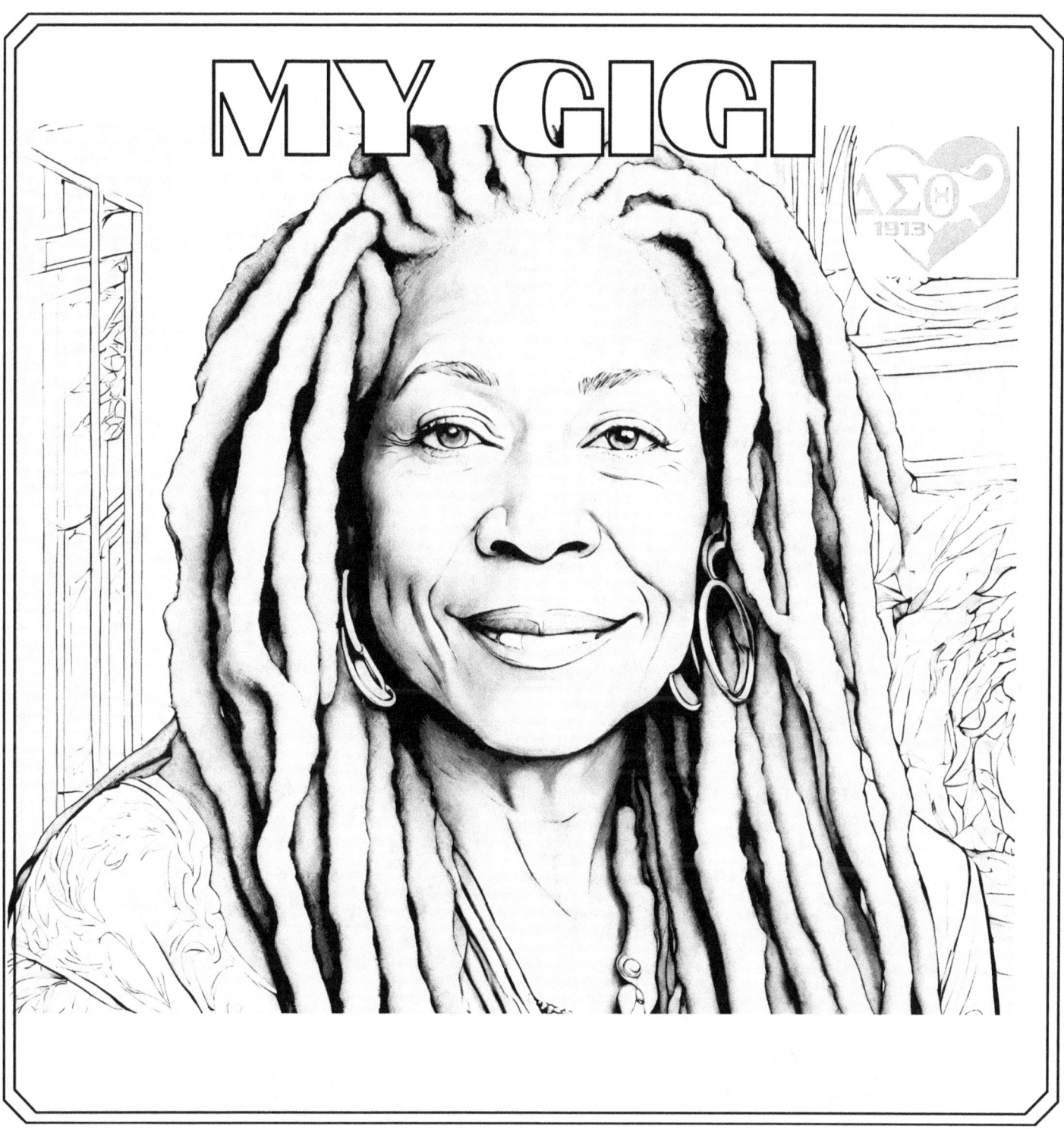

MY POP POP

THEY HAVE 2 DAUGHTERS

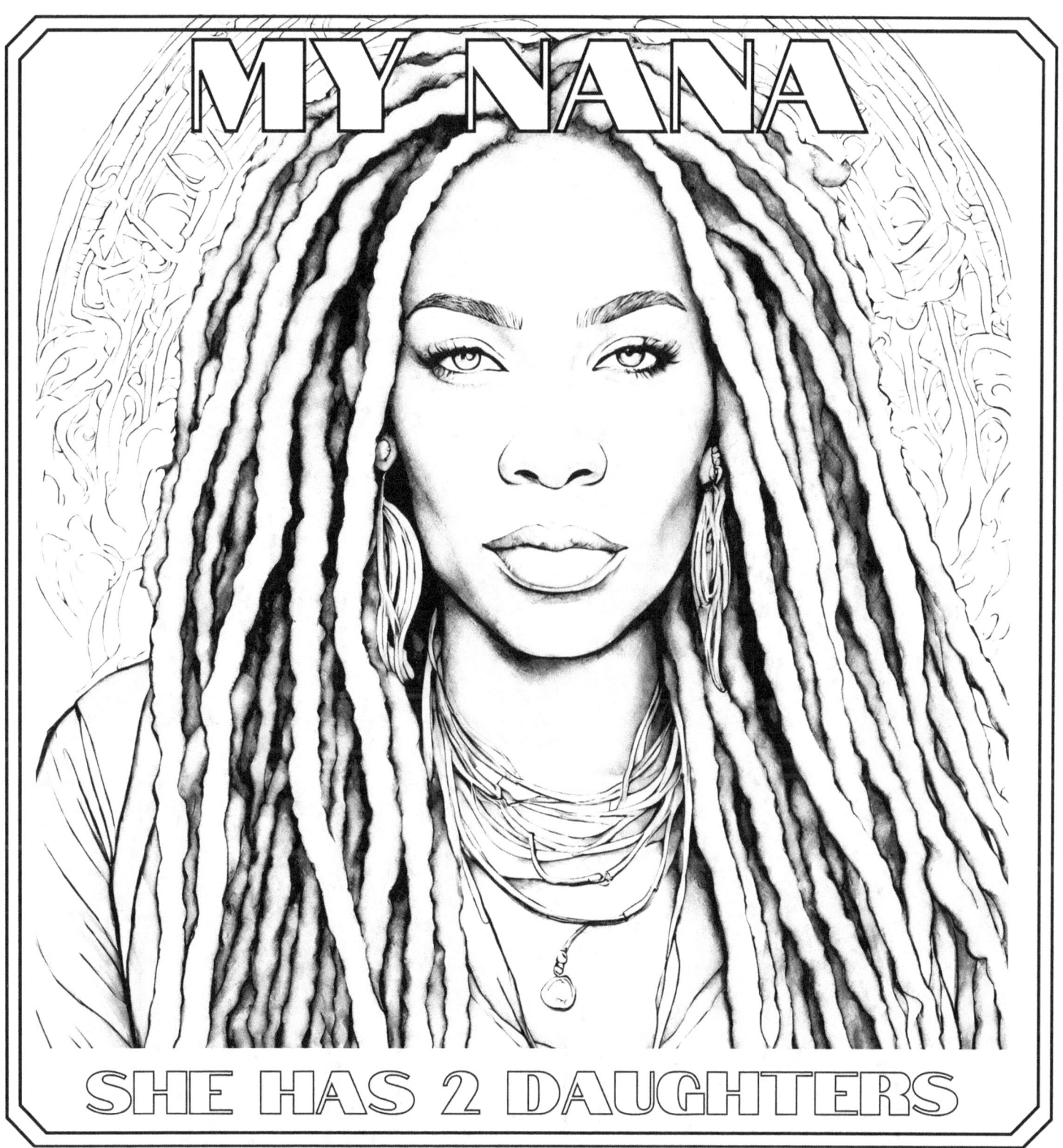

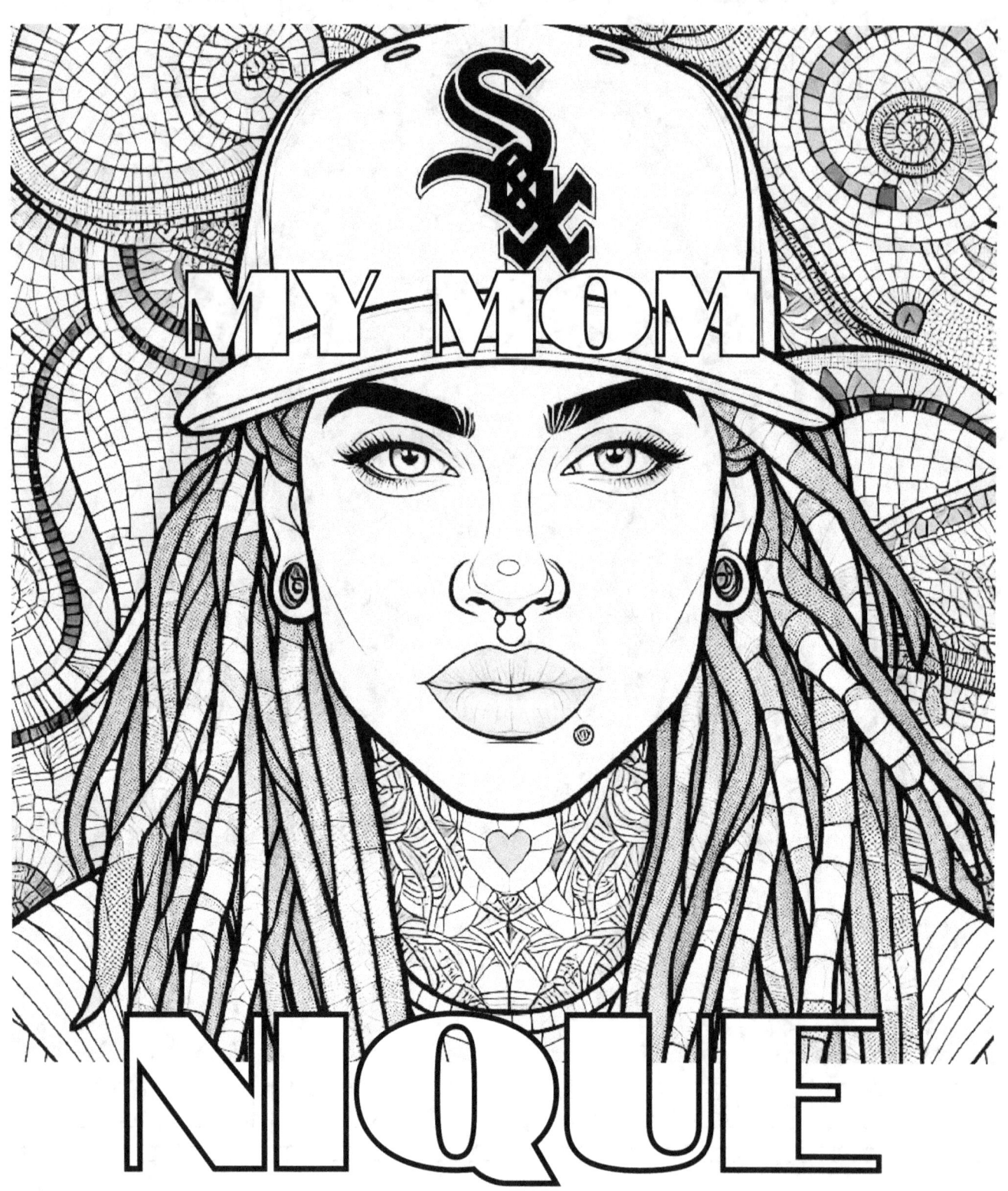

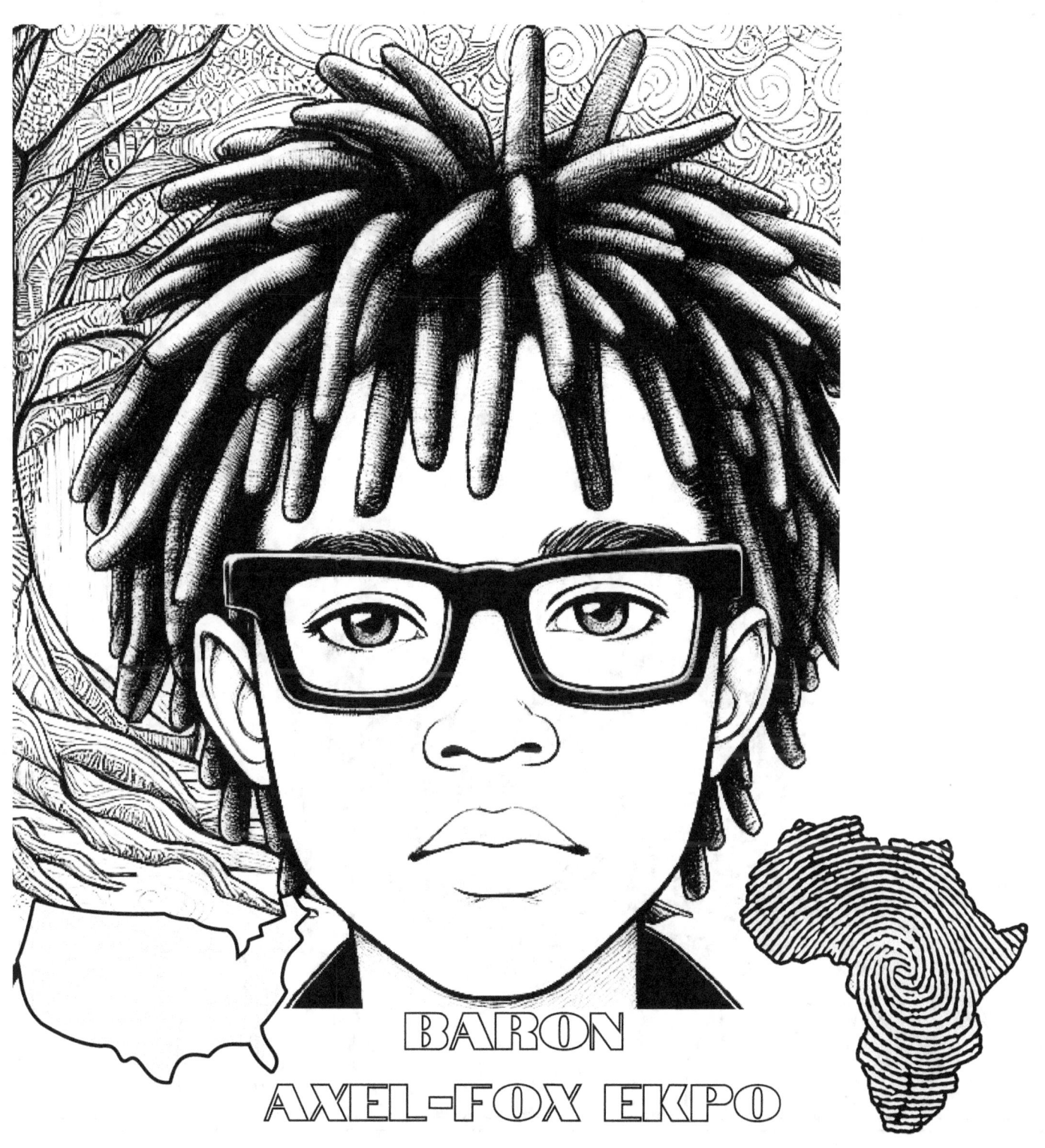

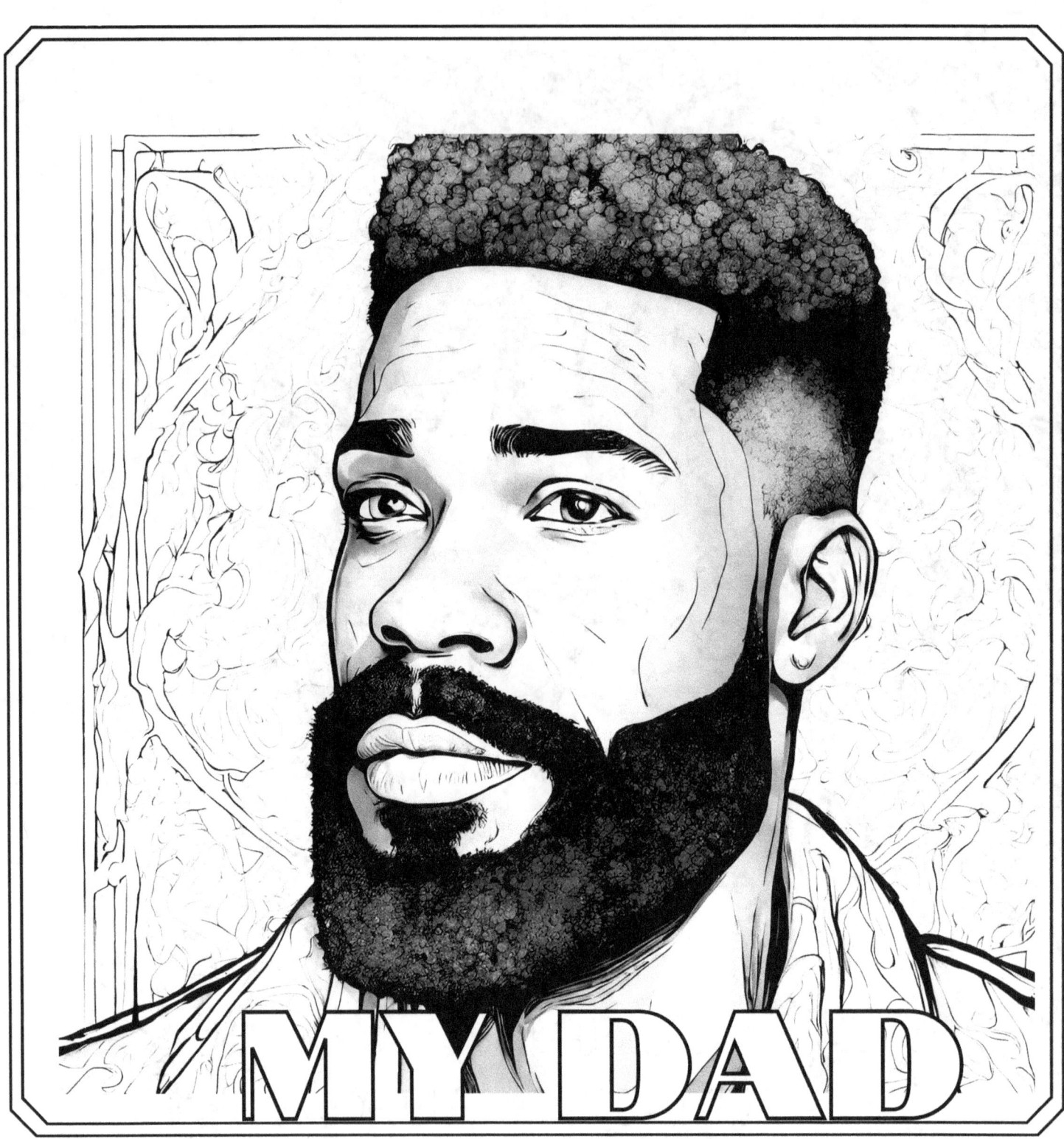

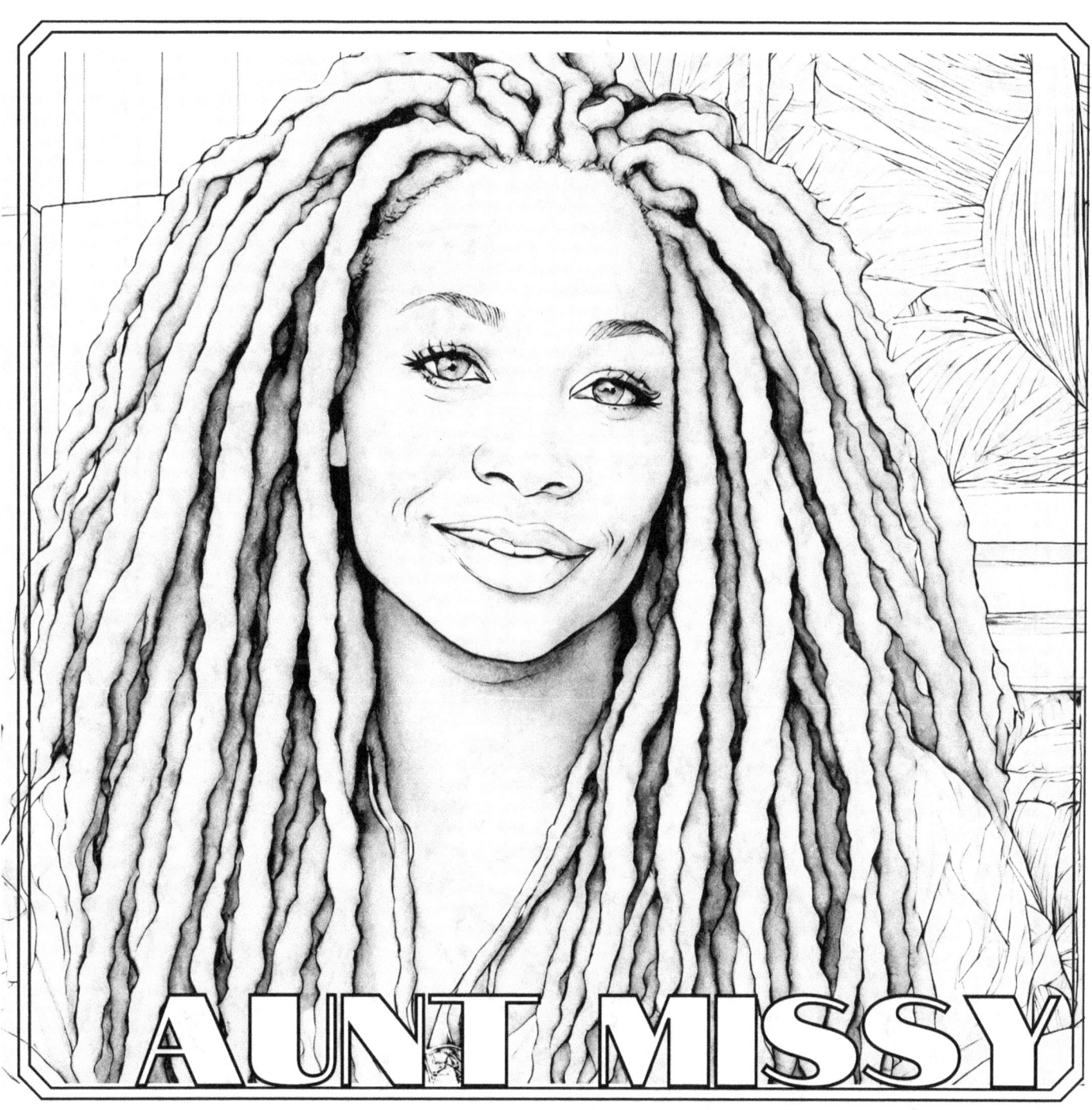

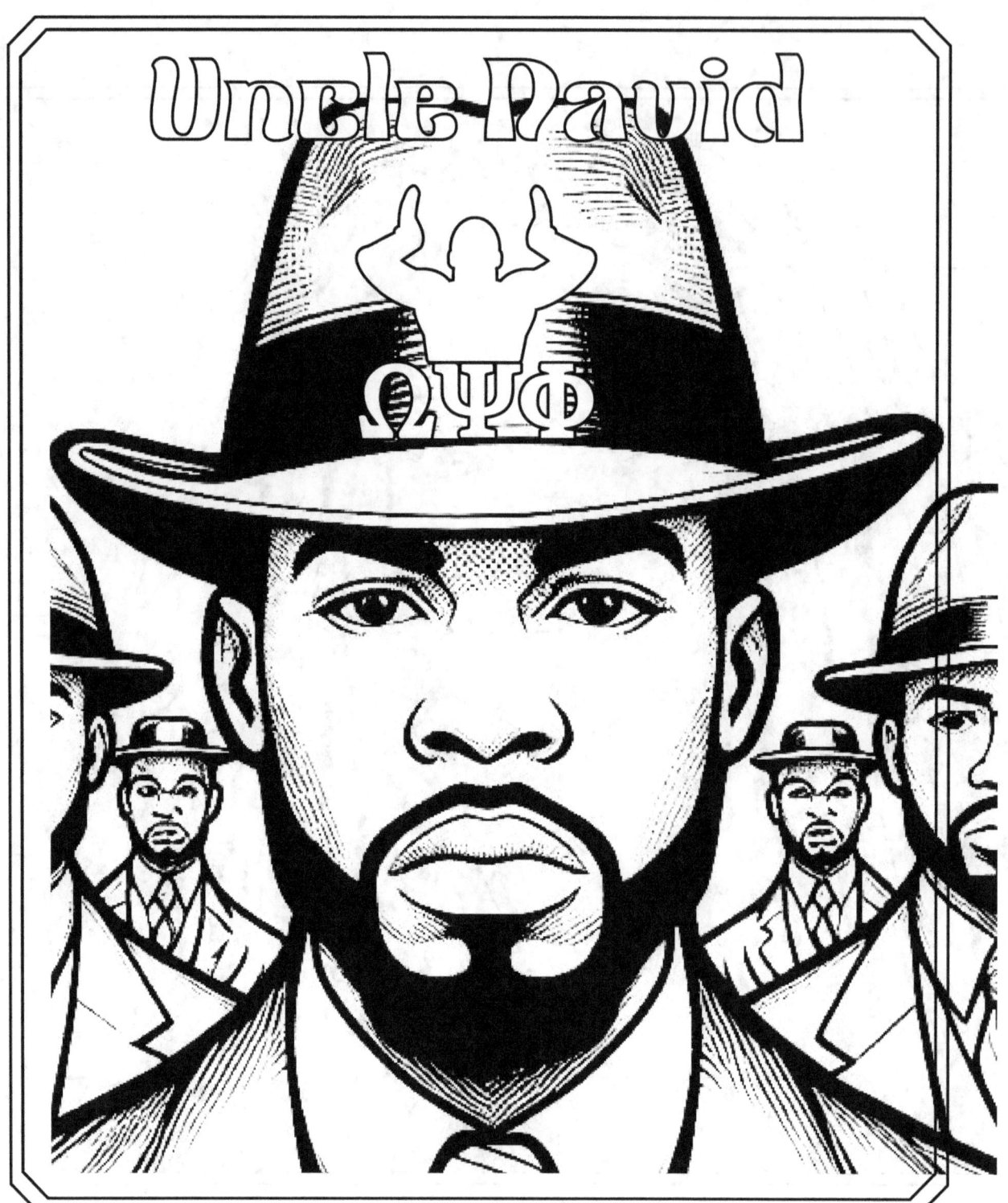

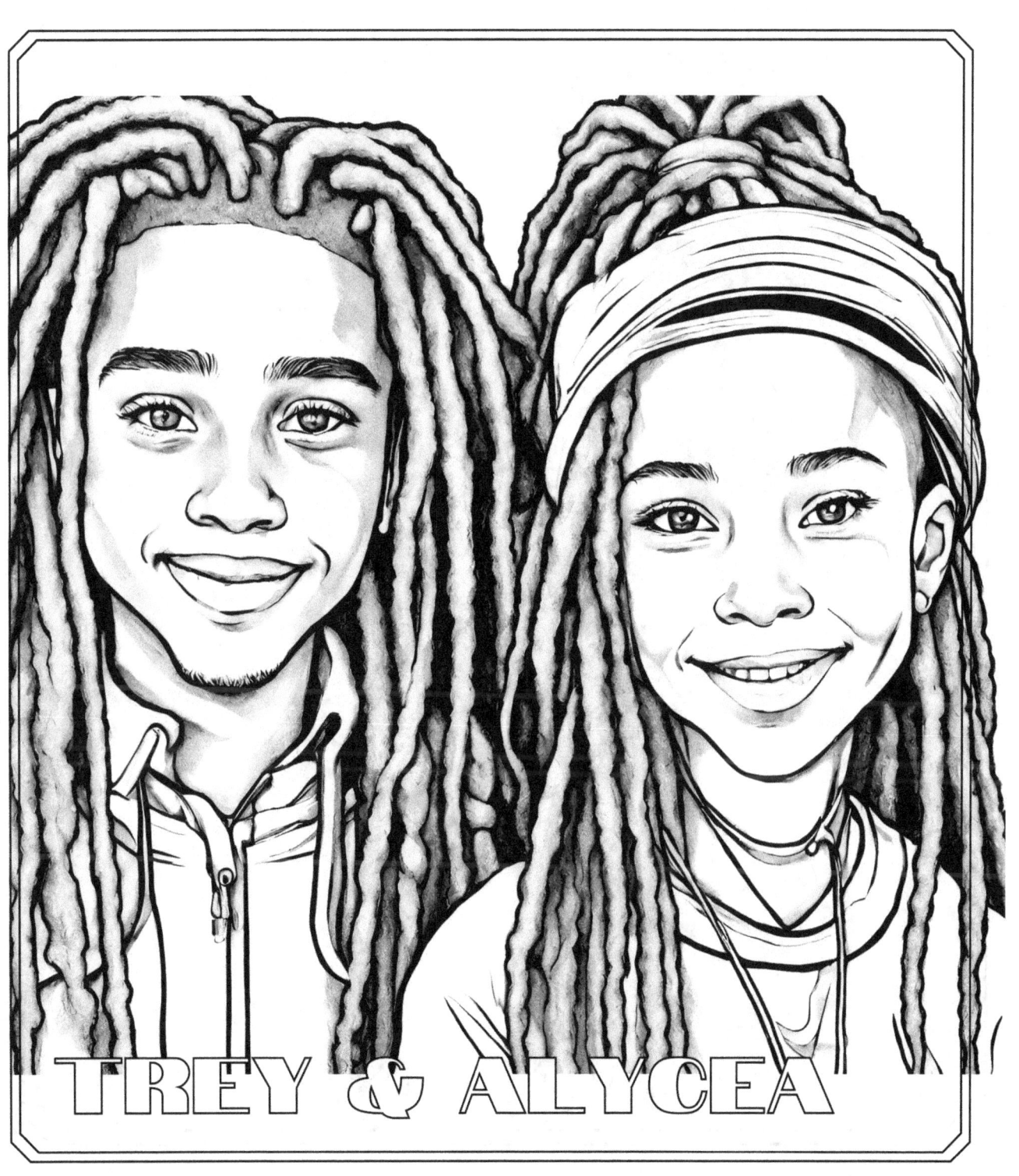

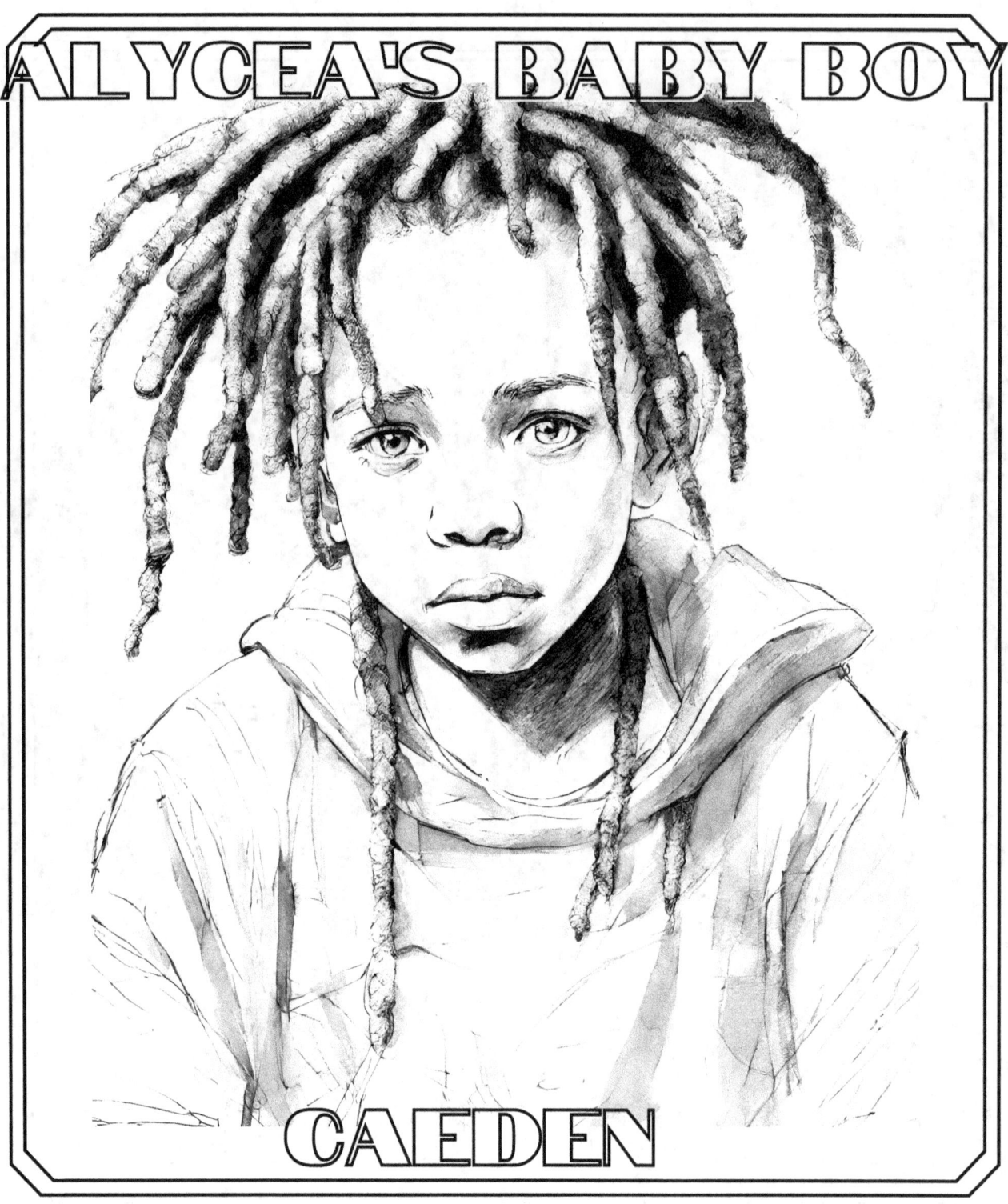

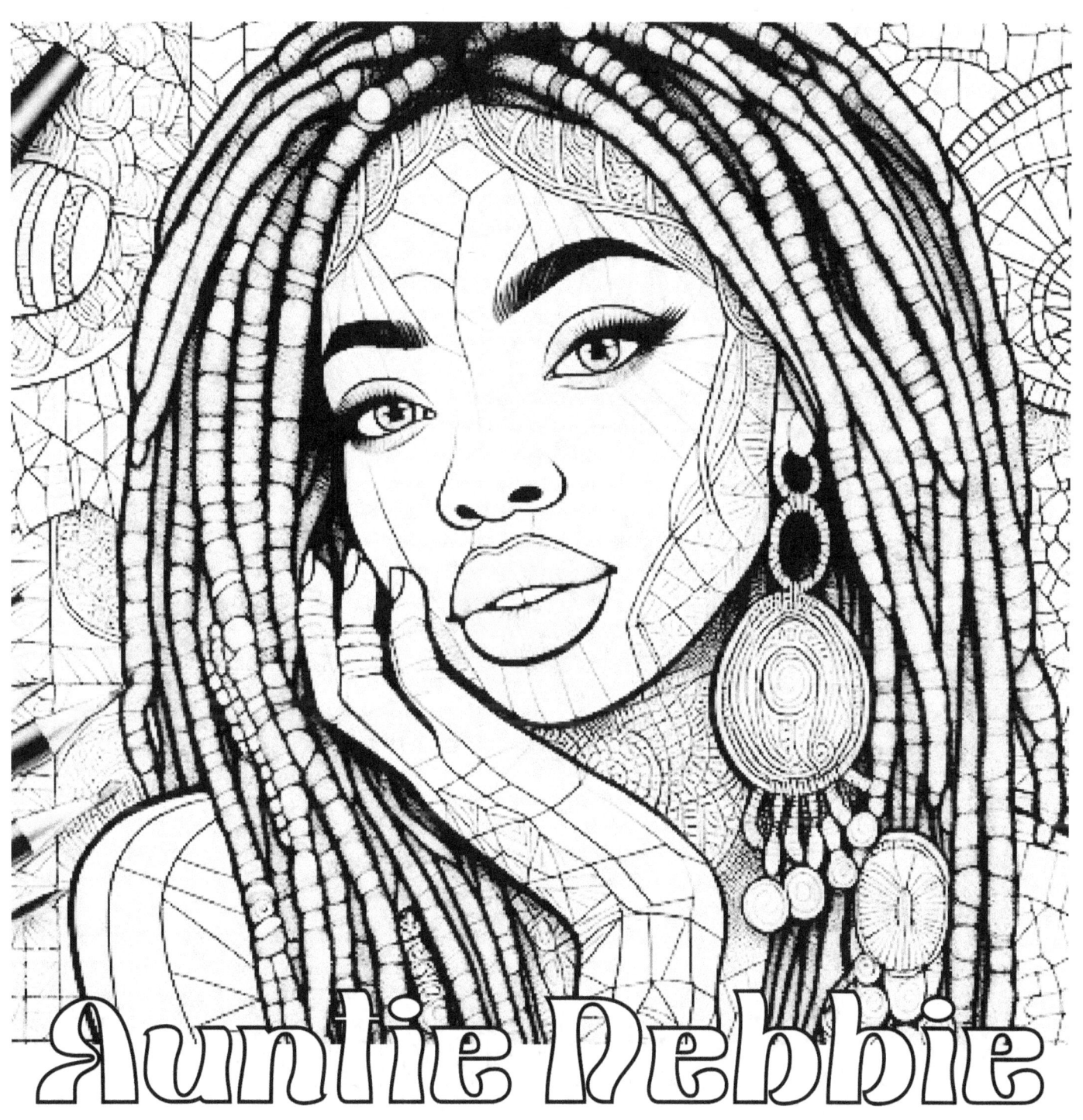

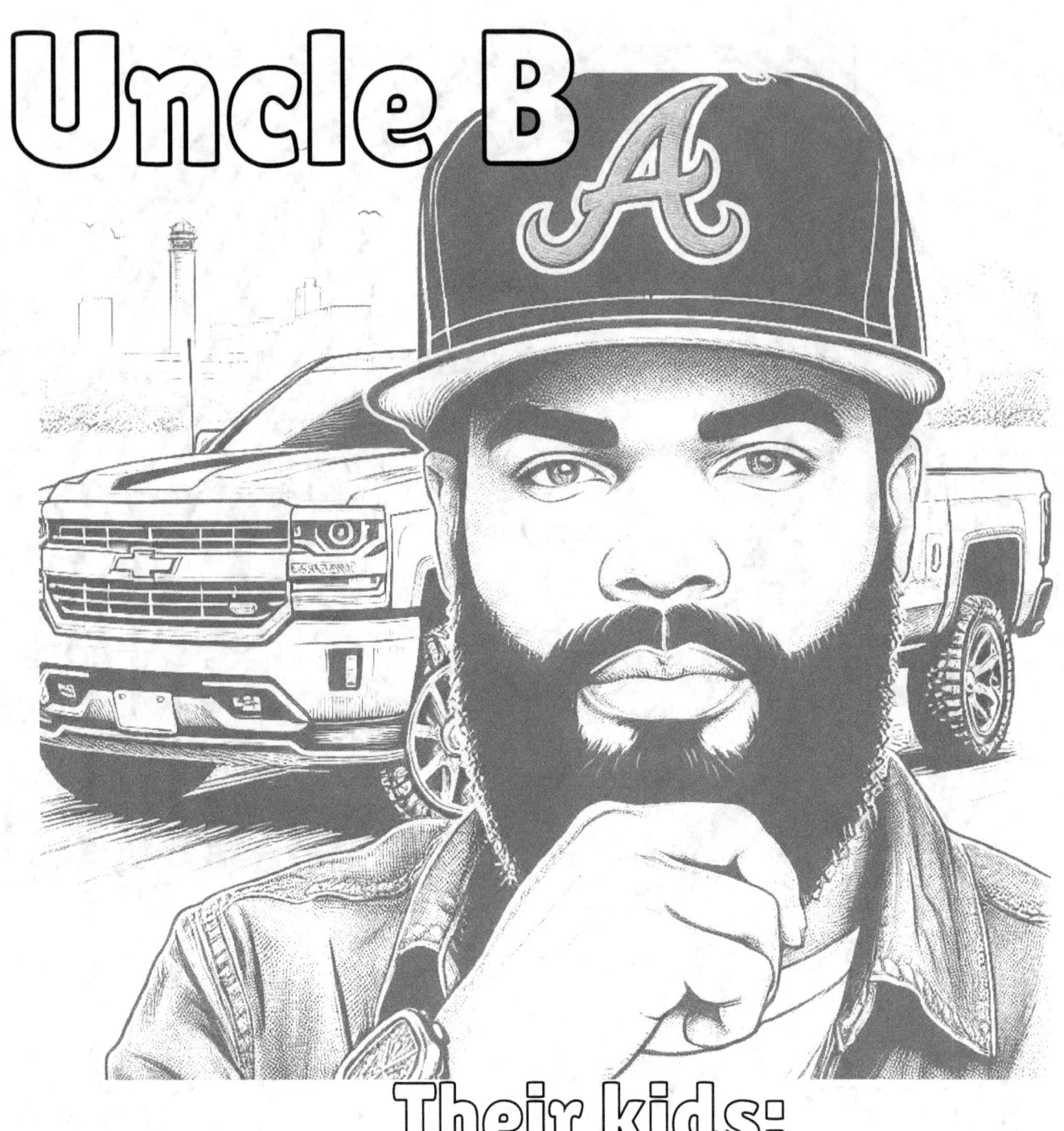

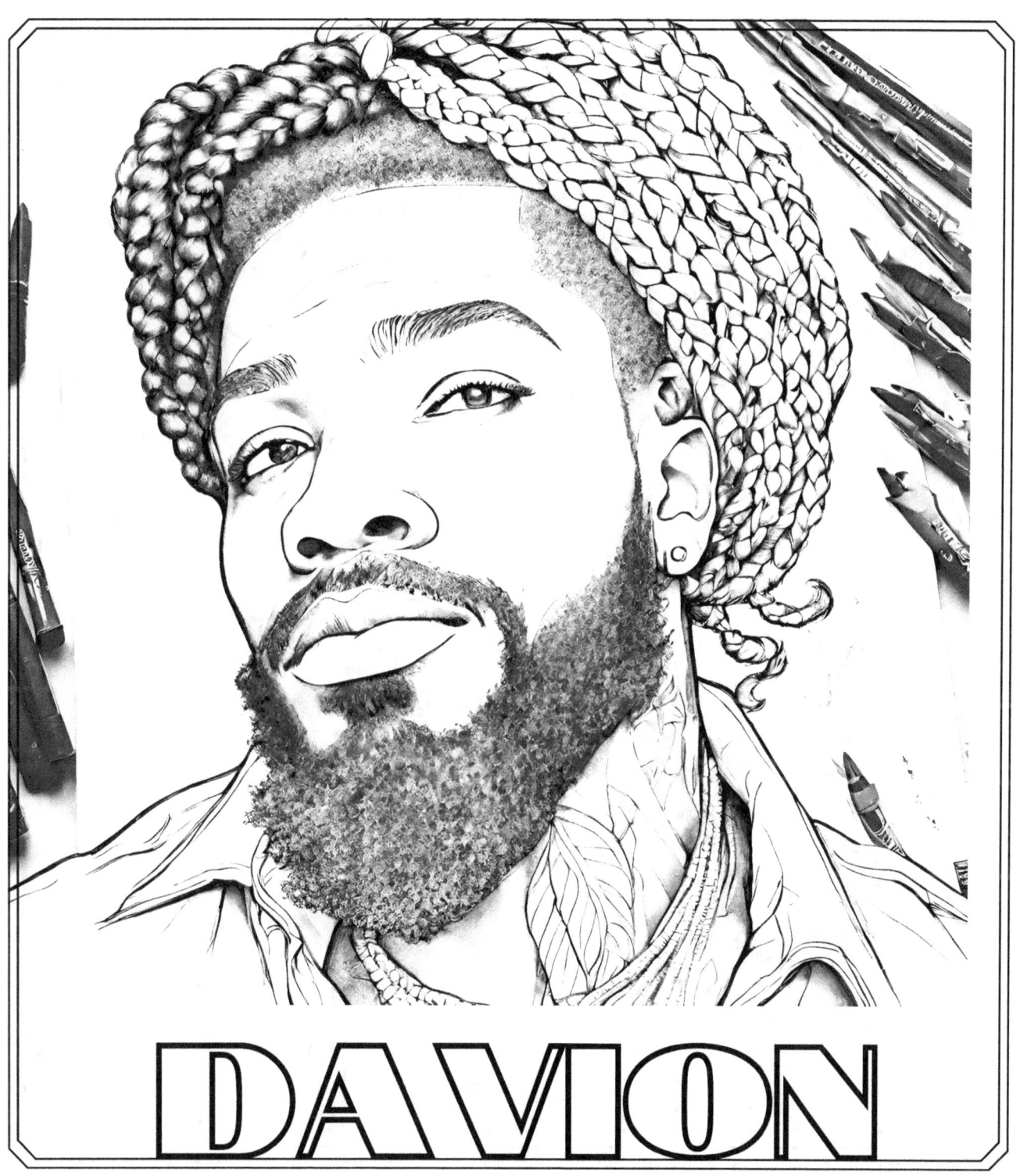

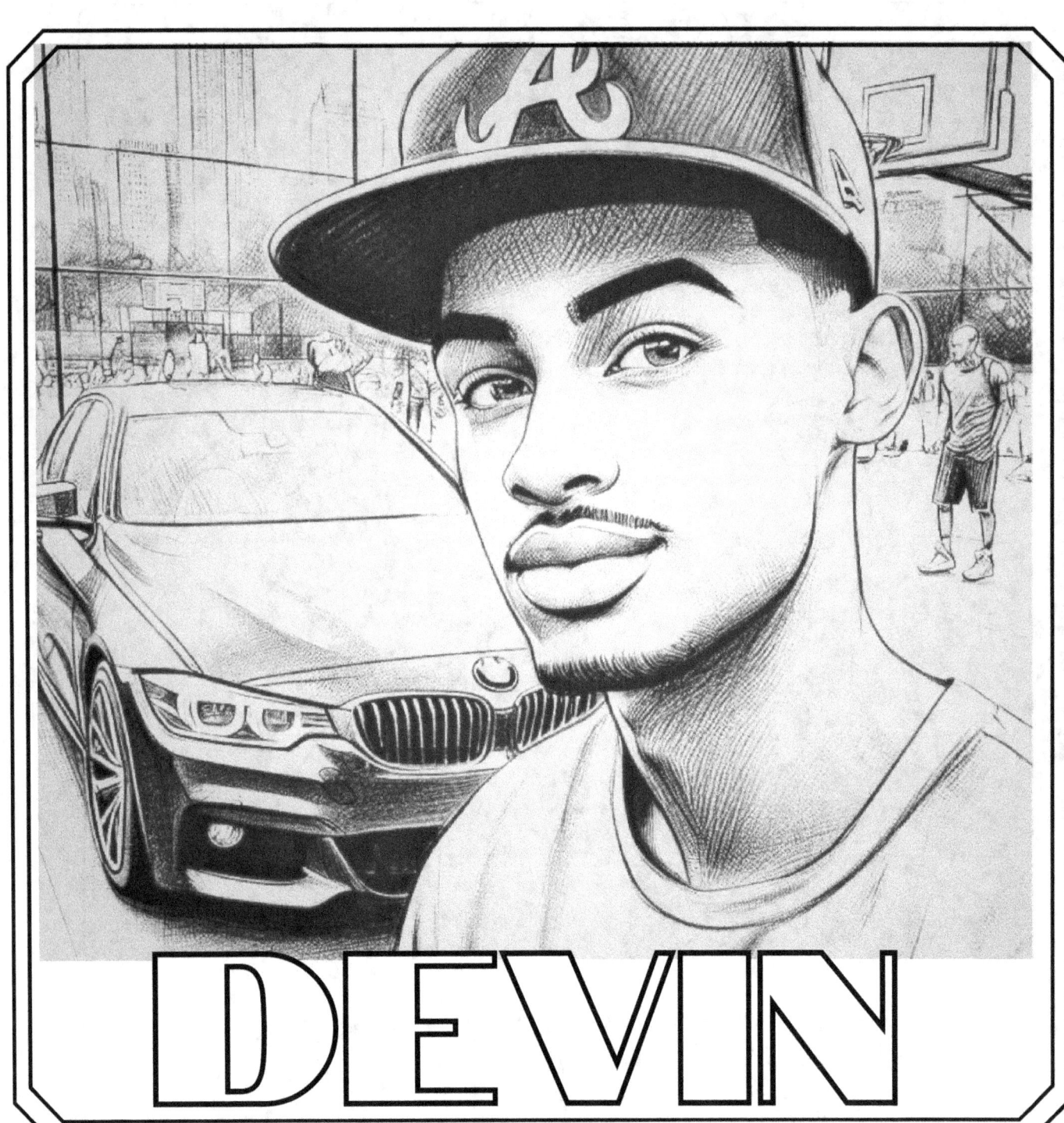

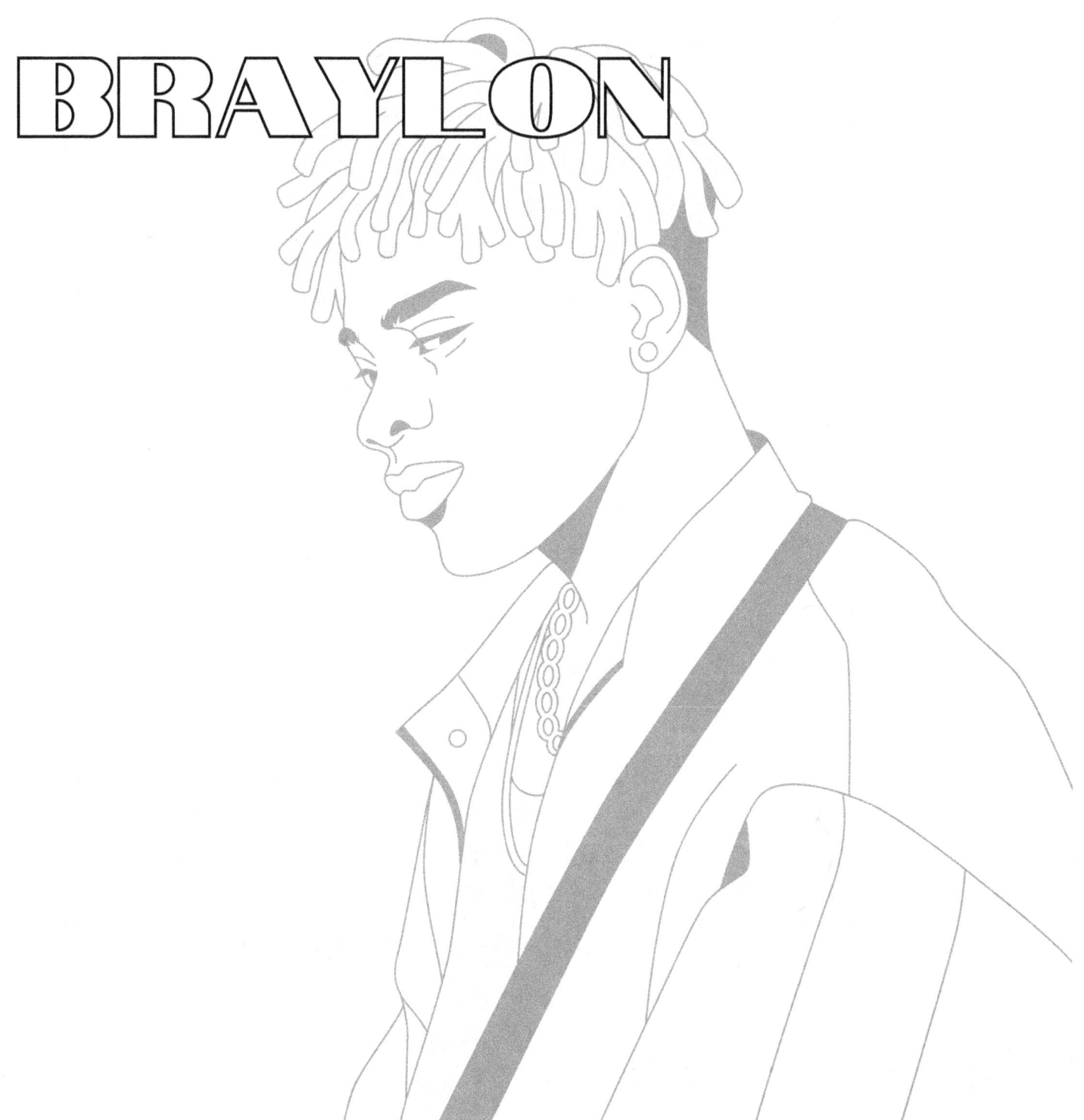

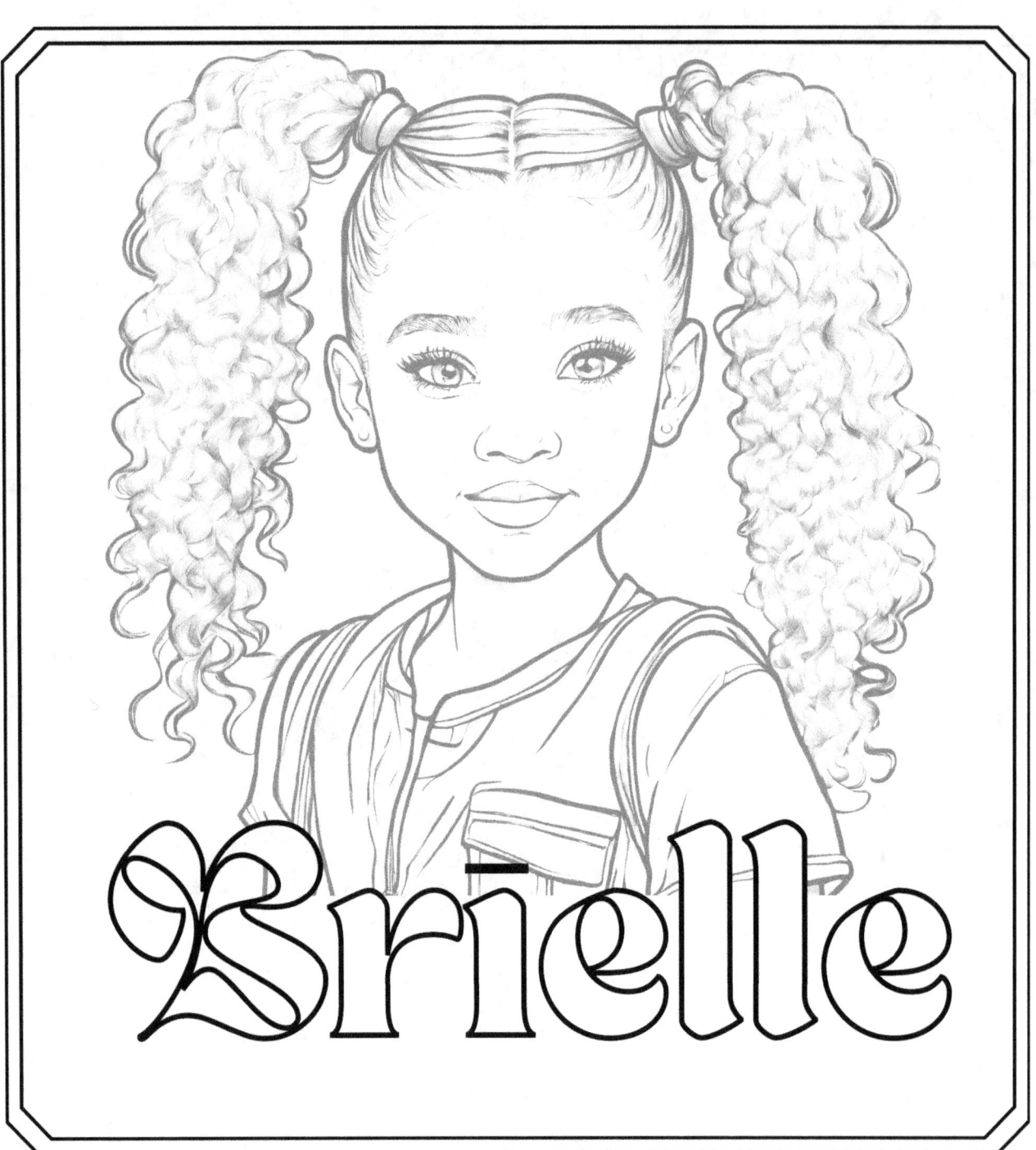

FAMILY ROOTS RUN DEEP, LIKE A TREE PLANTED IN...

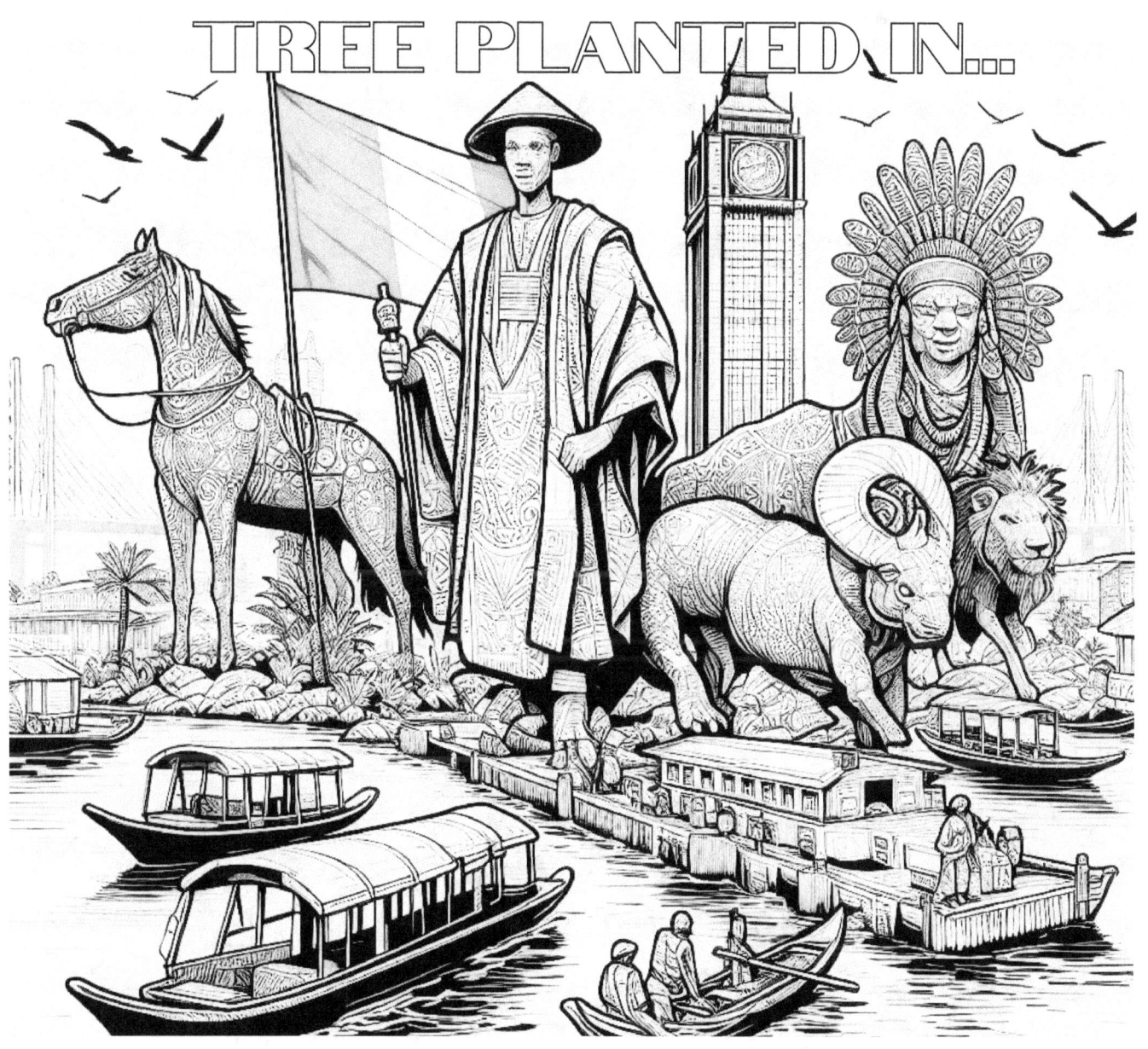

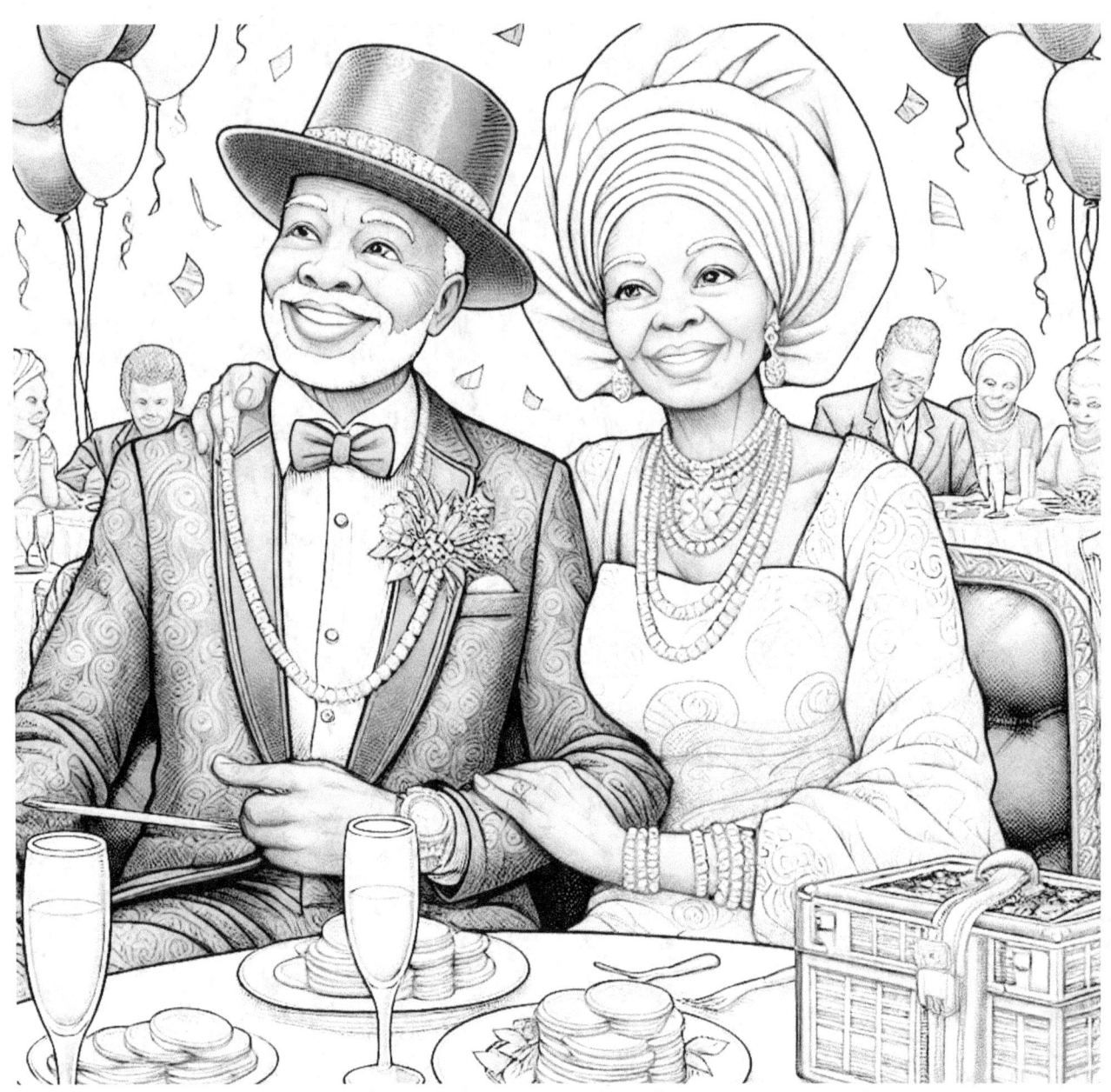

PAPA AND MAMA E ARE MY GRANDPARENTS

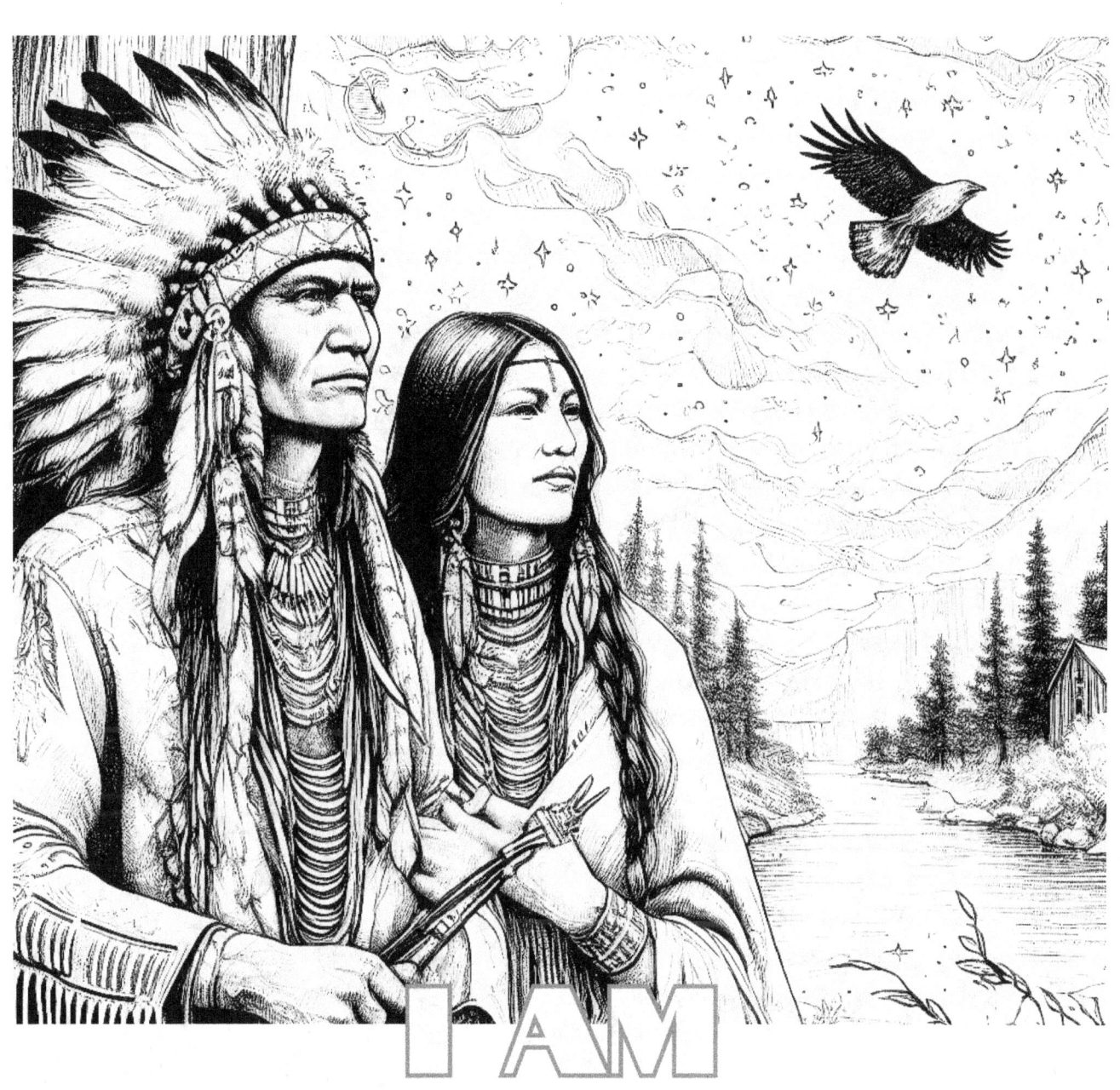

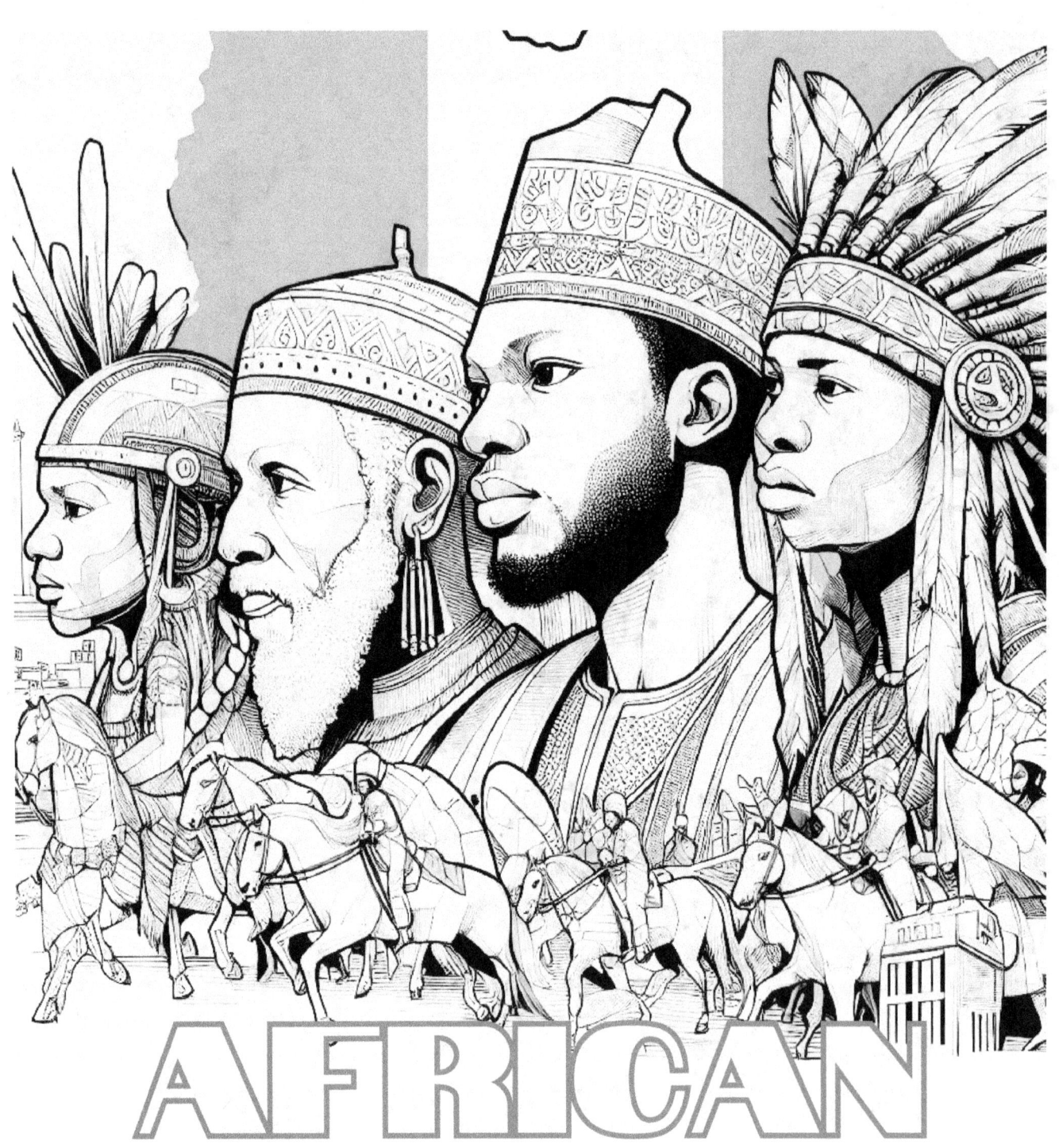

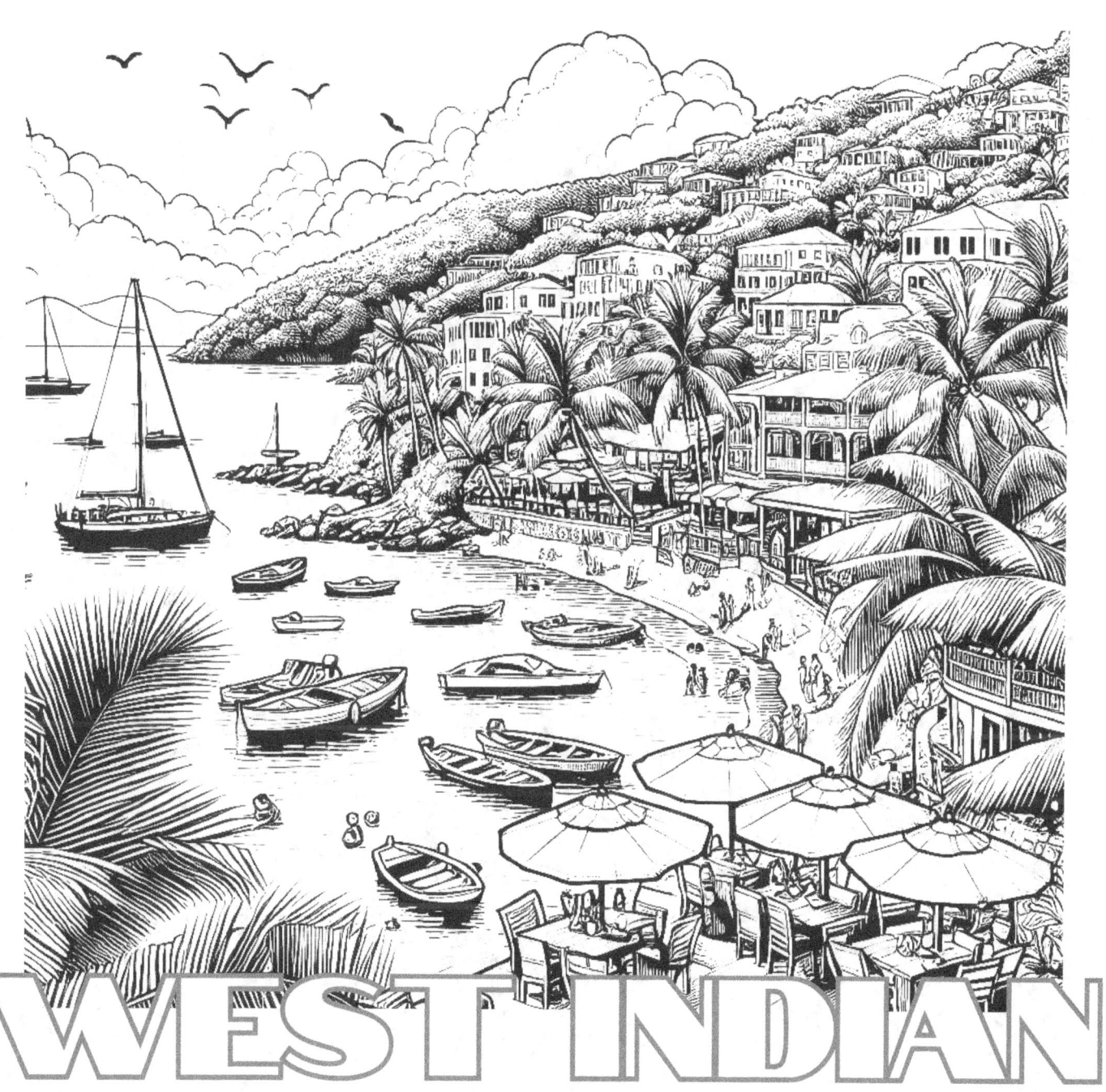

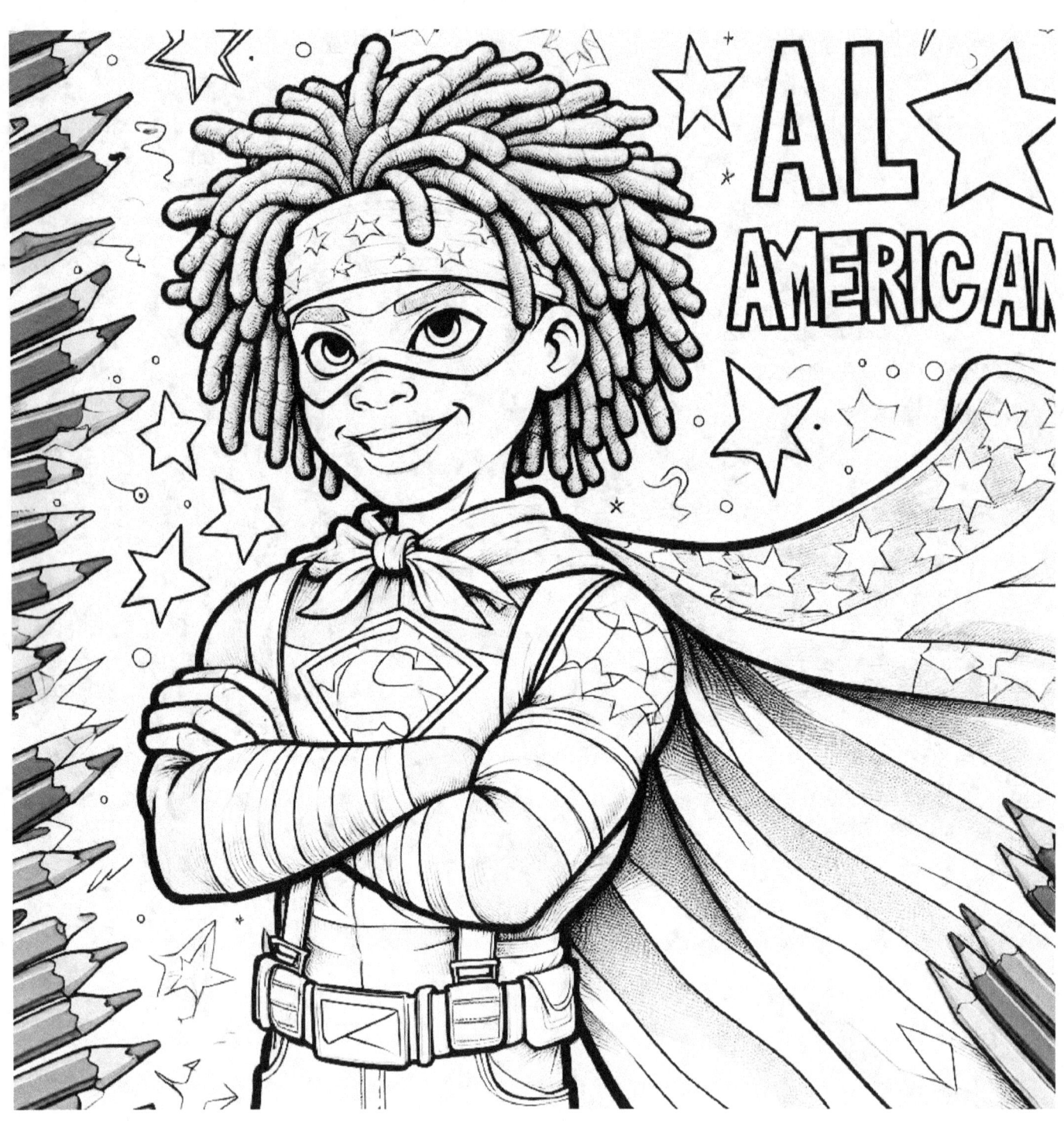

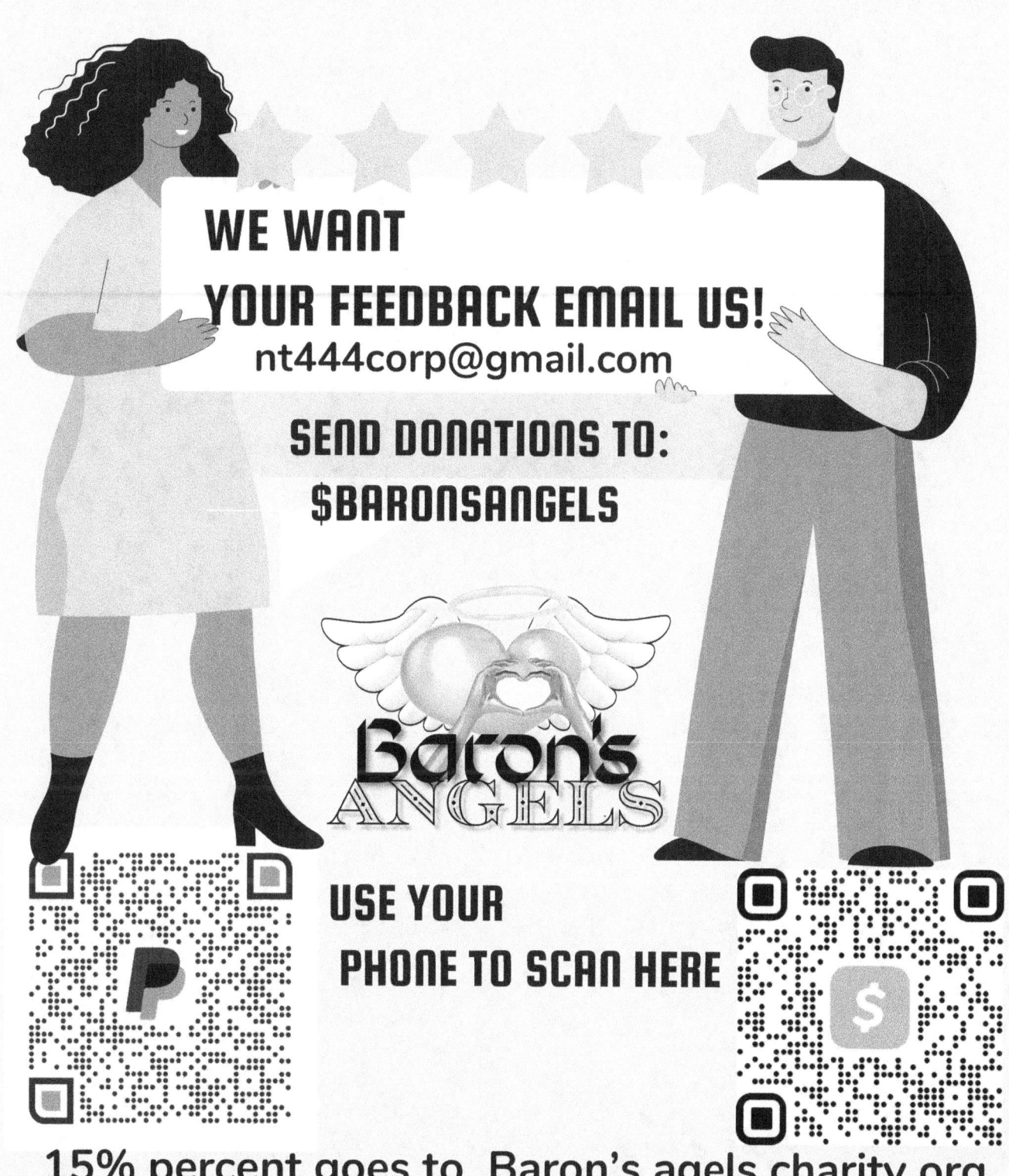

www.ingramcontent.com/pod-product-compliance
Lightning Source LLC
Chambersburg PA
CBHW082225220526
45470CB00010B/3308